SONGBIRDS

Written by Shelton H. Shelton

Illustrated by Paige P. Byrne

Look for this feather at the end of the book. There you will find inspiring discussion questions.

Visit our website **songbirdscreations.com**.
Follow along on Instagram @**songbirdscreations**
and **SongbirdsCreations** on Facebook.

Crippled Beagle Publishing
Knoxville, Tennessee
dyer.cbpublishing@gmail.com
(865) 414-4017

Printed in the United States of America
Book design by Marcy Gooberman

Copyright © 2020 Shelton H. Shelton and Paige P. Byrne
Hardcover ISBN 978-1-970037-45-6
Paperback ISBN 978-1-970037-55-5
Library of Congress Control Number: 2020919529

*En memoria de Sara,
madre muy cariñosa y amiga de muchos.*

*In Memory of Sara,
loving mother and friend to many.*

Dedicated to the friendship of Chip and Jacob

*Also to all of our little songbird nieces and nephews:
Abbi, Adan, Asahel, Bo, Chloe, Cooper, Cora, Coston, Elise Paige,
Lauren, Lily Anna, Marion, Olivia, Tiffany, Tim, and Tripp.*

Sing the song God has put in your heart, and you will change the world.

Have you ever asked
yourself what makes
your sweet heart sing?

Is it a person or a toy
or maybe a tree swing?

Do you like to be outside where the wind blows through your hair?

Maybe you like to read
all cozy in a chair.

One day you want ice cream and the next a salty chip.

This week you eat veggies
but the next you pitch a fit!

Today you may imagine you're exploring on a trip.

Then you dream you're sailing on a giant pirate ship!

So why does it matter
what you think or feel?

Is that green or blue, or
do you call it teal?

It matters because God formed you just perfectly from the start.

All the things you like so much are hints about your heart.

Everybody is different, just like the birds you see. Some are red or yellow…

...while others are purple or green.

Their food can be different too,
like worms or seeds or fish.

Pink flamingos love big shrimp and think they're just delish!

When you hear one songbird tweet, it will maybe sound okay....

"Ahem... Squaawkaphooey...

When several chirp in harmony
it brightens up your day.

Suppose you toot your horn
attempting to play a song.

By yourself the notes fall flat and just might sound all wrong.

But add a grand piano, violin, or beating drums.

Throw in a singer or flute, and maybe tap your thumbs.

Now the song sounds better,
like music to your ears.

Don't be shy. It takes all types, so let go of your fears!

For His Glory,
God formed you and
every living thing.

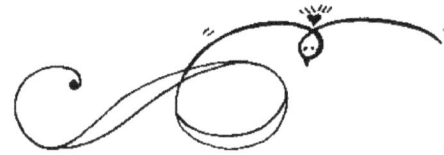

So ask Him to show you
ways to help Creation sing.

Because we're all so different, some days you may feel small.

You may feel your gifts don't matter and no one cares at all.

On those days remember
what puts a smile upon your face...

because those things you really like will help you find your place.

There are people all around you who might not understand...

God is **HUGE**, and we all have parts within His plan.

Each person is special,
with a part to play in life.

All pieces are important,
so be **YOU** with all your might!

Discussion Questions

What do you see when you look at different birds on these pages or in nature?

What experiences make your heart feel happy?

What are some of your favorite activities to do indoors and outdoors?

What foods did you like when you were young but dislike now? What kind of foods did you dislike when you were younger but like now?

When you are playing pretend, what world do you imagine?

What do you do when a friend likes something different than you do?

Why do you think God creates us to look different and like different things?

These birds in this story are from different parts of the world. How are they different, and how are they the same?

Families around the world eat many different foods. Tell me about something new you would like to try.

Do you know anyone who speaks a different language from the one you speak? Would you like to learn a new language?

What is your favorite song, and what makes you like it so much?

Would you like to play an instrument? Which instrument would you like to play? Why did you choose that instrument?

What do you notice about each of the children in this book?

You said that _____ makes you feel happy. How could you use that activity to do something good in the world?

What do you do to feel better on days when you have made mistakes?

How does God help people use their talents to bless others? What examples have you seen in your life?

How can you share God's love with others even if they have a different faith than you?

What are some ways you can help others be brave? How are you brave?

Ask God to show you how He made you to help Creation sing.

How a friendship helped write a story:

I remember being a timid child when I was very young. I was an observer, and it took a while to find my voice with others. My friend Paige and I went to the same church and school. My mom remembers how I would light up with a smile around my new friend. My friendship with Paige helped me become a bit more confident. Being able to laugh together brought out the best in both of us. I can still remember watching Paige draw and color at school. I was amazed by her natural abilities and maybe even a bit jealous! I longed to be really good at something, but I was not yet sure what that was. I participated in many activities, but those things never made my heart sing. Paige and I began to go our separate ways because our interests were different, but we still remained friends and could always make each other laugh. Paige pursued her God-given gifts as an artist and continues to bless children with her talents as an art teacher. Eventually, I started studying the Bible and the life of Jesus on a deeper level and began participating in and leading Bible studies. I became less focused on myself in prayer and began to look around for ways to bless others. This shift in thinking is really where my life took on a whole new meaning. I started journaling and realized that there were many thoughts and ideas in my head that needed to get out. When I wrote this story, there was no question about whom I wanted to illustrate it.

-Shelton H. Shelton

Readers, learn about Chip and Jacob:

My son Chip and his friend Jacob were born barely one month apart and lived just down the street from one another. When they started kindergarten, Chip was shy and nervous because he did not know anyone in his class. Jacob was also nervous because he was not yet confident in speaking English. Jacob remembers liking Chip because he thought his name was cool and it was easy to say. Chip liked Jacob because he came right up to him and introduced himself. From there a friendship was born. Chip did not have any idea that Jacob came from a different culture. In fact, the boys used to pretend they were brothers. Jacob's mom died when he was in second grade. When we heard, our family went to theirs in support. My husband and I felt nervous because we were not sure how we would be received. What we found was that we had much to learn from them about hard work, respect, loyalty, and hospitality. By walking alongside a family in their grief, we gained a whole new perspective on life.

The boys now attend different schools and participate in different sports. We go to church together and see each other as often as we can. Chip says Jacob is one of the most trustworthy people he knows. We have become extended family, and we found a few additional "aunties" to help along the way. Our hope is that this book will open up conversations with children about their own gifts and talents and encourage them to bravely be who God created them to be. When we embrace the way we were uniquely created, it becomes easier to see value in others.

I encourage everyone to walk alongside different types of people and listen to their stories like Jesus did. Let's all be quick to listen and brave to speak up for what is right. Like the sounds you hear from different birds in the trees or how each instrument works together to form an orchestra, "We all work together to help Creation sing."

-Shelton H. Shelton

Shelton Haynes Shelton and her husband Rick reside in Knoxville with their son Chip and dog Lexi. Shelton graduated with a degree in Bachelor of Arts in Communications from The University of Tennessee. She worked for 18 years in TV and radio advertising sales. She loves being a mom and tía (aunt) to her adopted and biological nieces and nephews. She has always enjoyed reading and has several book ideas in the works.

Paige Preston Byrne and her husband Geoff reside in Savannah, Georgia, where they are both employed by schools in Savannah and own Scribble Art Studio. Paige is currently working on her Masters of Fine Arts in Painting at Savannah College of Art & Design. She received her Masters of Art in Art Education from GW: Corcoran School of the Arts & Design in 2014. She has won numerous awards, including a Portfolio Thesis Award in Publishing an eBook and is the recipient of the 2013 District of Columbia Mayor Arts Award for Excellence in Teaching of the Visual Arts.

www.ingramcontent.com/pod-product-compliance
Lightning Source LLC
Chambersburg PA
CBHW041101070526
44579CB00003B/32